KT-522-444

FOOD IN FOCUS

Cakes and Muffins

Author

Haze

C 04 0092708

First published in Great Britain by Heinemann Library
Halley Court, Jordan Hill, Oxford OX2 8EJ,
a division of Reed Educational and Professional Publishing Ltd.

Heinemann is a registered trademark of Reed Educational
and Professional Publishing Ltd.

OXFORD FLORENCE PRAGUE MADRID ATHENS
MELBOURNE AUCKLAND KUALA LUMPUR SINGAPORE TOKYO
IBADAN NAIROBI KAMPALA JOHANNESBURG GABORONE
PORTSMOUTH NH (USA) CHICAGO MEXICO CITY SAO PAULO

© Reed Educational and Professional Publishing Ltd 1999

The moral right of the proprietor has been asserted.

All rights reserved. No part of this publication may be reproduced, stored in a retrieval
system, or transmitted in any form or by any means, electronic, mechanical,
photocopying, recording, or otherwise without either the prior written permission of
the Publishers or a licence permitting restricted copying in the United Kingdom issued
by the Copyright Licensing Agency Ltd, 90 Tottenham Court Road, London W1P 0LP.

Designed by Celia Floyd
Illustrations by Barry Atkinson, pp. 13, 14, 20, 21, 22, 23, 24, 26, 28;
Oxford Illustrators, pp. 18, 19
Printed in Hong Kong

03 02 01 00 99
10 9 8 7 6 5 4 3 2 1

ISBN 0 431 08884 5

British Library Cataloguing in Publication Data

King, Hazel
    Cakes and muffins. - (Food in focus)
    1.Cake - Juvenile literature 2.Muffins – Juvenile
    literature
    I.Title
    664.7'5

WEST DUNBARTONSHIRE LIBRARIES		
C040092708		
CBS		21/02/200?
J641.865		£5.99
		BH

This book is also available in hardback (ISBN 0 431 08877 2).

Acknowledgements

The Publishers would like to thank the following for permission to reproduce
photographs:

Gareth Boden, pp. 4, 7, 8, 10, 15 bottom, 16, 17, 22, 25, 27, 29;
Chris Honeywell/Hayden Bakery pp. 12, 13, 14, 15; Zefa, p. 5 (Ed Rock).
Werner Forman Archive, p. 6.

Cover photograph: Trevor Clifford

Every effort has been made to contact copyright holders of any material reproduced in
this book. Any omissions will be rectified in subsequent printings if notice is given to
the Publisher.

Contents

Some words are shown in bold, **like this**. You can find out what they mean by looking in the Glossary.

Introduction

Tempting and delicious

If you look in a cake shop or along the cake shelves in a supermarket it is easy to see why people choose to buy these sweet treats. They are designed to look tempting and taste delicious – so much so that one of them is rarely enough!

Cakes may be iced or plain, full of fruit or filled with jam and cream. They may be large or small, round or square and come in many different flavours and colours. Whatever they are like, they always contain sugar or a sweetener – and that is why people like them!

As sweet as sugar

Today many of us have rather a 'sweet tooth' – we enjoy eating sweet foods. The problem is, sugar is not very good for us. You will find out more about sugar on page 17.

As long as we don't eat too many of these sugary foods, it can be enjoyable to eat something sweet, such as a chocolate chip muffin or a slice of gingerbread. These foods are usually eaten because we like them, not simply to fill us up.

A colourful display of cakes and muffins

There are many different occasions when we prepare or buy sweet foods for our family and friends to enjoy. We often eat a special cake on somebody's birthday. Today we can choose from some really exciting designs in the shops. Some cakes can be specially prepared with a name or a message piped on top.

This girl is enjoying a slice of birthday cake

Other occasions when we have special cakes include weddings, anniversaries, christenings, Easter-time and other religious celebrations.

Food served at parties is often a mixture of sweet and savoury dishes. Savoury foods include crisps or potato chips, sandwiches, samosas or pies. At children's parties the sweet foods usually include different types of cakes and they are often brightly decorated to appeal to children.

Cakes are a great way to raise money too. Fêtes, bazaars and fairs all have cake stalls selling home-made cakes. Baking and selling cakes is fun – and a good way to raise money for charity as well!

Cooking as a pastime

People must eat food to survive. Food provides us with all the important **nutrients** that make up our bones, muscles and skin. Today we have many different foods to choose from, and this makes eating fun and enjoyable. However, this has not always been the case.

Early people

When early people first roamed the earth they knew they had to find food to survive. To them, 'food' meant fruits, berries or cereal grains, plants that grew naturally all around but had to be found and picked. Early people also killed animals which were then eaten raw. This may sound unpleasant today but that was how human beings survived on earth long ago.

Just as we experiment with different ingredients and recipes today, so early people tried out new ways with food. For example, they found that by mixing grains with water they could make a type of porridge. Many ideas were probably discovered by accident!

Experimenting with food in this way gave people a more varied diet, which helped increase their chances of survival. Of course, once fire had been discovered food could actually be cooked, producing new tastes and flavours.

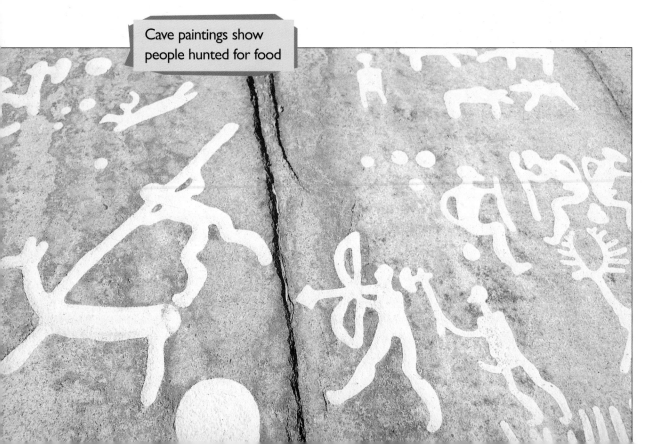

Cave paintings show people hunted for food

Gradually, as people became more advanced, food – and eating – became more interesting. Different countries tended to have their own styles of preparing, cooking and serving food. This included cakes and other sweet foods.

Cakes developed at different times in different countries but they were generally served after the meat dishes had been eaten. People were no longer eating just to survive but because they liked eating.

Cakes from the past

In India, during the 1600s, round dough cakes were made using *ghee* (a type of fat) and stuffed with flour, almonds, honey and sesame oil. On top of each one was a brick-shaped sweet cake made of flour, sugar and ghee.

At about the same time in France, **confectioners** were selling gingerbreads and other cakes and by the 1700s sweet foods, such as puddings and cakes, were starting to appear in British recipe books.

Muffins were originally made by the early American settlers, although these should not be confused with English muffins which are flat and made with yeast. There is still confusion today between the American and English muffin!

American and English muffins are very different products

Cakes of the world

There are thousands of different types of cakes. Many of them are known to come from a particular place or country.

United States of America

Angel food cake is a very light cake made without using any fat. It is decorated with white frosting and is said to be the 'food of angels'!

Australia

Lamington is an Australian small cake named in honour of Lord Lamington, Governor of Queensland from 1895 to 1901. Lord Lamington's cook is said to have created the cakes by dipping a square of buttercake in chocolate icing, then coating it with a chocolate icing glaze and rolling it in coconut.

Mediterranean *Halva* and *Baklava*

Mediterranean countries

Halva is made from sugar, butter, semolina and roasted nuts or sesame seeds. It may be flavoured with spices, such as saffron, cinnamon or cardamom.

Baklava is a sticky cake made from layers of a pastry called filo and filled with ground nuts, sugar and spice. A sweet syrup is poured over the baked *baklava*.

Central and western Europe

Paris Brest is a famous French gâteau designed in 1891 to celebrate the bicycle race from Paris to Brest. It is made with a special pastry (choux) and filled with fresh fruits and cream.

Boter loek, traditionally from Holland, is a buttercake, cut into squares or fingers and flavoured with ginger and almonds.

Black Forest Gâteau, named after Germany's Black Forest, is a rich, chocolate cake decorated with chocolate curls, cherries and fresh cream.

Germany's rich, chocolatey Black Forest Gâteau

Princess cake is a sponge cake from Denmark which contains cream, custard and marzipan.

Pashka is a cake that was served in Russia during Easter-time. It is made from curd cheese, dried fruits and nuts and is shaped like a pyramid.

Sacher torte was designed in 1814 in Vienna, Austria. It is a rich, light chocolate cake covered in an apricot and chocolate glaze.

Zug torte, named after the Swiss town of Zug, is a sponge cake flavoured with the liqueur, Kirsch.

Panforte di Sienna is a very flat, heavy, rich cake made with honey, spices and dried fruits. In Italy it is traditionally served in thin slices at Christmas.

United Kingdom

Battenberg cake was, at one time, called Tennis cake because its design looks a bit like a tennis court. It is made from squares of sponge, in different colours, then wrapped in marzipan.

9

Making cakes and muffins at home

Cakes

Cakes come in all shapes, sizes and flavours. One reason why there is so much variety is because different methods are used to make cakes.

The methods can be divided up as follows.

Creaming method

Basic ingredients

- 100 g soft margarine or butter
- 100 g caster sugar
- 2 eggs
- 100 g self-raising flour

Basic method

1 **Cream** (beat) the fat and sugar.
2 Beat in the eggs, one at a time, with 1 tablespoon of flour.
3 Gently **fold** in the remaining sieved flour.

Rubbing-in method

Basic ingredients

- 75 g block margarine or butter
- 200 g self-raising flour
- 75 g caster sugar
- 1 egg
- water or milk to mix

Basic method

1 Rub the fat into the flour, stir in the sugar.
2 Add the egg and milk and mix to a soft dough.

Melting method

Basic ingredients

- 75 g margarine or butter
- 50 g brown sugar
- 75 g black treacle
- 75 g golden syrup
- 200 g plain flour
- 1 level teaspoon bicarbonate of soda
- 1 egg
- 2 tablespoons milk

Basic method

1 Melt the fat, sugar, treacle and syrup together in a pan.
2 Sieve the dry ingredients into a bowl.
3 Pour the melted ingredients, egg and milk into the bowl. Mix to a smooth batter.

Whisking method

Basic ingredients

- 50 g caster sugar
- 2 eggs
- 50 g self-raising flour

Basic method

1 Whisk the eggs and sugar together.
2 Sieve the flour and fold it into the mixture.

Muffins

Muffins are a bit unusual because although the method is always more or less the same, the varieties seem endless! Traditionally muffins are an American recipe and are eaten at any time of the day. They may be sweet or savoury.

Making muffins

Basic ingredients

- 225 g plain flour
- 100 g caster sugar
- 2 teaspoons baking powder
- pinch salt
- 1 egg
- 250 ml milk
- 120 ml oil

Basic method

1 Mix the flour, sugar, baking powder and salt together in a bowl.
2 Mix the eggs, milk and oil together in a jug. Pour the liquid into the dry ingredients, folding them in quickly.

Flavour ideas

- Lemon and sultana
- Courgette (zucchini) and Parmesan cheese
- Breakfast bran
- Chocolate
- Blueberry
- Apple and custard
- Banana and peanut butter
- Apricot and pecan
- Chocolate chip

A variety of flavoured American muffins

Muffins should be light and well risen. Baking powder is used in the recipe to make them rise during baking. It also helps if the flour is sieved twice. Air is trapped in the flour as it falls from the sieve, and this makes the muffins light.

Another thing to remember when making muffins is to fold the dry ingredients quickly into the wet ones. The mixture should not be beaten or stirred (don't worry if it looks lumpy!). This helps to keep the muffins light.

Making cakes for the shops

When cakes are made to be sold in shops, they have to be made in very large quantities. This means the equipment must be big enough to hold all the ingredients. The method of making them may also change.

People who work with food must not let any dirt or germs get onto the food, so they wear protective clothing. The pictures show a chocolate fudge cake being made for sale in a shop.

1 The raw ingredients are delivered to the food manufacturers. Some are stored at room temperature and some are chilled.

▼

2 The dry ingredients are weighed and packed into a plastic container with the recipe attached. They are sent to the bakery where the chilled ingredients are weighed. The dry ingredients are blended with the fats in a huge mixer.

▼

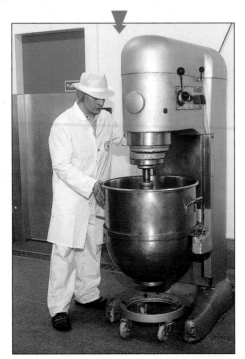

3 The rest of the ingredients are mixed together, then added to the mixer. Sometimes the machines have to be stopped and the sides scraped by hand.

▼

4 The cake batter is poured into a hopper. The hopper is designed so the batter pours out through nozzles, straight into greased tins below.

▼

▼

5 The cake tins are placed on baking racks inside the large rack oven. A turntable inside ensures that the cakes cook evenly. They are baked at 190°C for 30 minutes.

6 After baking, the racks are taken out and the cakes are cooled. They are moved to a storage area and taken out of their tins.

7 Next, the cakes go to the 'high care finishing department'. For **hygiene** reasons this area has a different set of staff, a special air flow system and is kept at 12°C.

8 As the cakes pass along a conveyor belt, the tops are trimmed with a cutting tool called a mandolin.

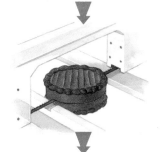

9 Some fudge icing is poured onto each cake base from a nozzle. The top is added and the whole cake is put on a cake card.

10 Skilled cake decorators spread more fudge icing over the sides and top using a palette knife. Then they pipe on a decoration.

11 The finished cake is placed in a strong cardboard box showing the date and a number. The cakes are put on plastic delivery trays and chilled very quickly to 2–4°C. This is called **blast chilling**.

12 The cakes pass through a metal detector before being stacked and covered with plastic. They are loaded onto the lorry which is sealed with an airlock so they always stay chilled.

13 If a chocolate fudge cake leaves the manufacturers at 10 o'clock one evening, it could be sitting in the supermarket by 7.30 the next morning!

The finished cake

Choosing ingredients

Although there are lots of different recipes for cakes and muffins, some ingredients are used quite a lot. These ingredients include:

- flour
- fat
- sugar
- eggs.

For any food product that is made, the ingredients are always chosen for a particular reason. For example, eggs can be whisked, or they can be beaten, and the results will be different. A Swiss roll is a very light sponge because the eggs have been whisked. In a fruit cake, the eggs are beaten into the mixture so the result is not as airy.

The main ingredients for cakes and muffins

The ingredients chosen for cakes and muffins will depend on their **function** – or what they are able to do. Here are some of the functions of the main ingredients in cakes and muffins.

Flour

Flour forms the main **structure** of the food product. Self-raising flour helps the product to rise. Soft flour or cake flour is used to make most types of cakes and muffins. Soft flour is low in protein which helps to give a fine, even **texture**.

The flour may be white, wholemeal or wheatmeal.

These flours may also be either self-raising or plain.

Self-raising flour	Plain flour
Baking powder is added to make the finished product rise.	Baking powder is not added.

Fat

Fat has several functions. It:

- adds colour and flavour
- helps the food to keep longer
- traps air, making the product light
- makes the product moist and/or rich.

Beating or **creaming** fat with sugar helps to trap air bubbles. This is why Madeira cakes, for example, rise. Muffins and cakes, such as gingerbread, use melted fat or oil because they are not beaten in the same way. Cakes, such as rock buns, have fat rubbed into the flour.

Sugar

There is a wide variety of sugars available. Sugar:

- adds a sweet flavour
- helps produce the right texture
- helps trap air, when beaten with fat
- adds colour.

Eggs

Eggs also have several functions. They:

- trap air if they are whisked or beaten
- add protein
- add colour and flavour
- help the mixture to set when cooked.

When used in making cakes or muffins they may be beaten, whisked or used to **bind** dry ingredients.

icing sugar

honey

caster sugar

maple syrup

dark brown sugar

Some of the many types of sugars available

But are they good for you?

Cakes and muffins are usually eaten as a treat because they taste so good. People don't normally think about the **nutrients** they contain.

Nutrients are substances found in all foods that are used by our body after the food has been digested. The five main nutrients are:

- protein
- carbohydrate
- fat
- minerals
- vitamins.

Water is also vital for a healthy body.

Our bodies need to have these five nutrients, in the right amount, every day.

What do nutrients do?

Protein is needed to make our bones, muscles, skin and hair form properly.

Carbohydrate is divided into three types:

- sugars give us lots of energy
- starches give us energy and are found in foods like potatoes, rice, pasta and flour
- **dietary fibre** helps us to get rid of our body's waste material. It is found in foods containing bran as well as oats, pulses, fruits and vegetables.

Fat is needed in small quantities. It provides energy and vitamins.

Fatty foods supply vitamins A, D, E and K. Vitamins are found in lots of different foods and have many **functions**. For example, vitamin A is needed for good night vision, healthy skin and tissue.

Minerals are very important to our bodies and they are found in lots of foods. For example, iron is needed to keep our blood healthy. It is found in egg yolk, dried fruit and wholegrain cereal.

blood cells

Nutrients in cakes and muffins

As we have already seen, the main ingredients used to make cakes and muffins are flour, fat, sugar and eggs. The nutrients they contain give the food its **nutritional value**.

Flour

Flour is made by milling cereal grains, for example, wheat, rice and maize. It provides starch (carbohydrate). Wheat flour is often used for baking and contains some protein, calcium and vitamins B_1, B_2 and B_3. Flour supplies about 340 kcal/1420 kJ per 100 g.

Fat

Fat supplies about 750 kcal/3140 kJ per 100 g. Fat also provides vitamins A, D, E and K.

Sugar

There are several different types of sugar:

- sucrose (from sugar cane and beet) is often used for cakes and muffins
- fructose is found in fruits and honey
- lactose is found in milk and milk products.

These last two types are found naturally in foods. Cakes or muffins that have had these ingredients added to them will contain these sugars too.

Eggs

Eggs contain yolk and white. Fat is found in the yolk. Eggs also provide protein, vitamin A, vitamin B_1, B_2, B_{12}, folic acid and iron. A hen's egg supplies about 80 kcal/335 kJ.

The 'healthy diet pyramid'

Healthy choices

For our bodies to work properly we need to have some food every day. However, if we are not careful about our choice of food and the amount we eat, we could end up being unhealthy or even unwell.

To help us make healthy choices when we eat, foods can be put into different groups. By looking at these food groups we can easily see which foods we should eat only occasionally, which foods we can eat regularly and those that are somewhere in between.

This 'healthy diet pyramid' helps us make the right choice about the food in our diet.

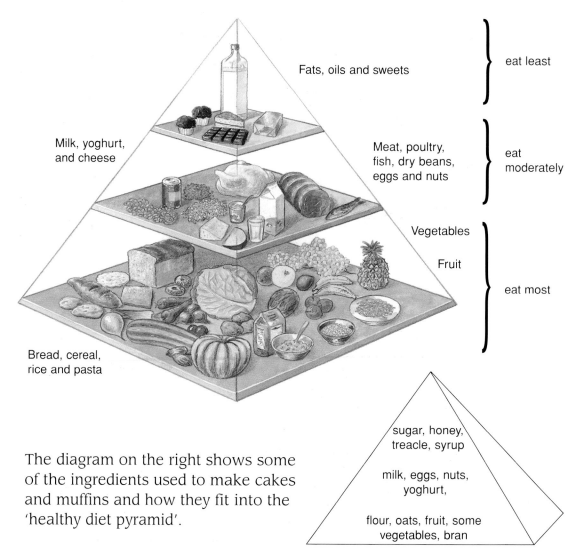

Fats, oils and sweets — eat least

Milk, yoghurt, and cheese

Meat, poultry, fish, dry beans, eggs and nuts — eat moderately

Vegetables

Fruit

eat most

Bread, cereal, rice and pasta

sugar, honey, treacle, syrup

milk, eggs, nuts, yoghurt,

flour, oats, fruit, some vegetables, bran

The diagram on the right shows some of the ingredients used to make cakes and muffins and how they fit into the 'healthy diet pyramid'.

How does the 'healthy diet pyramid' work?

To have a healthy diet, we should choose foods in the same proportion as they appear in the 'healthy diet pyramid'. That is, most foods we eat should come from the bottom of the pyramid, some should come from the middle and just a few from the top.

The 'eat most' foods are healthy for us because they are low in fat, sugar and salt and they provide **dietary fibre** to help our digestive system. They are quite filling foods but are not too high in calories.

The 'eat least' foods are those that are linked to health problems. The chart below shows how today's scientists believe certain foods affect us.

Food	Possible harmful effects	What to do
Salt	Too much salt may cause high blood pressure in some people. This means the heart is being overworked.	Do not add salt to meals or cooking. Do not eat too many snacks, such as crisps, nuts, etc.
Sugar	Eating too many sugary foods can lead to tooth decay and becoming overweight.	Choose sweet foods only as a treat. Clean your teeth after eating sugary foods.
Fat	Animal fats are thought to cause heart disease. Animal fats include butter, lard, fat on all meat, dairy products and eggs. Eating too many fatty foods may make you put on weight.	Instead choose vegetable oils and margarines, low-fat dairy products, fish, chicken and turkey without skin.

Experimenting with raising agents

Most cakes and all muffins need a **raising agent** to make them rise when they are baked. They need to be well risen to make sure they are soft and light to eat.

Raising agents form bubbles of gas inside the cake or muffin mixture. Then, as the mixture gets hot, the bubbles get bigger, making the cakes or muffins rise.

Cakes and muffins have a soft, light texture

How can air be used as a raising agent?

Experiment – trapping air in flour

You will need:

- 1 small glass
- bag of flour
- tablespoon
- 2 large bowls
- sieve
- table knife

What to do:

1 Carefully fill the glass with flour. Keep patting it down until no more flour will fit in. Use a knife to make the top level with the rim of the glass.

2 When you are sure you cannot fit any more flour into the glass, tip the flour from the glass into a sieve resting over a bowl. Then, sieve the flour again, using the second bowl.

3 Now carefully refill the glass with the sieved flour. What has happened?

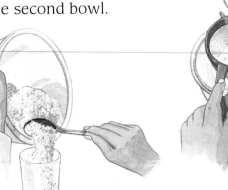

Conclusion

Air gets trapped in flour when it is sieved and this increases the volume of the flour. There are three ways to get gas bubbles into a mixture.

1 By including air – sieving the flour, beating the fat and sugar, and whisking the eggs and sugar will all add air.

2 By creating steam – adding liquid to a mixture means the water in it will turn to steam during baking.

3 By adding a raising agent – baking powder, bicarbonate of soda and self-raising flour (which contains baking powder) are all raising agents. They release tiny bubbles of **carbon dioxide** in the mixture making it rise.

Muffins rise during baking because they contain a lot of liquid and because baking powder is usually added. This means that they use two types of raising agent – steam and carbon dioxide.

Different kinds of cakes need different ways to make them rise. Devil's food cake, for example, is a rich, chocolate cake made by beating (or **creaming**) the butter or margarine with the sugar. The flour is sieved before being added.

Muffins

This recipe is for the American-style muffin which has a light **texture** and distinctive shape. Muffins are so popular in America today they even have their own web site! Before starting to cook, ask an adult to help.

American muffins

Makes 8–10

You will need:

Ingredients

- 225 g plain flour
- 2 teaspoons baking powder
- 100 g caster sugar
- pinch of salt
- 250 ml milk
- 120 ml sunflower oil
- 1 medium-sized egg

Equipment

- muffin cases
- 12-hole muffin tray
- scales
- sieve
- large mixing bowl
- medium-size bowl
- fork
- measuring jug
- mixing spoon
- tablespoon
- oven gloves

What to do:

1 Set the oven to Gas Mark 6 or 200°C. Put a muffin case into each hole in the muffin tray.
2 Sieve the flour and baking powder into a large bowl. Add the sugar and salt.
3 Pour the milk and oil into a medium-size bowl. Add the egg and mix together well using a fork. Pour into a measuring jug.
4 Make a dip in the middle of the flour using the mixing spoon, then pour in the liquid ingredients. Stir together until you can't see any flour. (You may see some lumps but don't worry about those!) This must be done carefully but quickly. If you mix the mixture too much the muffins will not be light and airy.

5 Using a tablespoon, fill each muffin case about $\frac{3}{4}$ full. If any mixture drips onto the tray, wipe it up before putting the tray in the oven.

6 Wearing oven gloves, place the muffins in the oven, near the top. Cook for 20–25 minutes.

7 Use oven gloves to remove the muffins from the oven. When cooked, the muffins will look a little brown and feel springy when gently pressed with a finger. Let them cool for a few minutes before removing them from the tray.

A plain American muffin with a light texture and special shape

Follow the method above but try these different flavourings:

Blueberry and lemon muffins

Add 200 g washed blueberries and the grated rind of half a lemon to the flour mixture.

Chocolate chip muffins

Use 175 g plain flour and 40 g cocoa powder (instead of 225 g flour), sieved together. Add 100 g chocolate chips to the flour mixture and $\frac{1}{2}$ teaspoon vanilla essence to the liquid mixture.

Breakfast muffins

Use 100 g wholemeal self-raising flour and 125 g plain flour (instead of 225 g plain flour). Use 75 g caster sugar (instead of 100 g). Add 100 g chopped dried (ready to eat) apricots to flour mixture and 1 tablespoon of honey to liquid mixture.

Cake faces

Have fun creating faces on these cakes! Some ideas about how to decorate the cakes are shown in the photo on the opposite page. The cakes can be plain or flavoured and could be made for a younger brother or sister's party! They are based on an English recipe for Queen cakes. In the past, they were sometimes baked in heart-shaped tins. Ask an adult to help before starting to cook.

Cake faces

Makes 10–12

You will need:

Ingredients

- 100 g soft margarine or butter
- 100 g caster sugar
- 2 eggs
- 100 g self-raising flour

Ideas for flavourings

- grated rind of 1 lemon or orange
- 25 g desiccated coconut or chopped nuts
- 30 g chopped cherries, chocolate chips, sultanas or dried fruit
- for chocolate cakes remove one tablespoon of flour and replace with one tablespoon of cocoa powder

Glacé icing for decoration

- 75 g icing sugar
- about $\frac{1}{2}$ tablespoon warm water or orange or lemon juice

Equipment

- cake cases
- bun tin
- scales
- knife
- medium-size mixing bowl
- electric mixer or mixing spoon
- small bowl
- fork
- tablespoon
- sieve
- teaspoon
- oven gloves

What to do:

1 Set the oven to Gas mark 4 or 180°C. Place 12 cake cases in a bun tin.
2 Put the margarine or butter into a medium-size mixing bowl with the caster sugar. Beat together using a mixing spoon or electric mixer until the mixture is pale and fluffy.
3 Break one egg into a small bowl and beat it with a fork. Add to the mixing bowl, together with one tablespoon of flour (after it has been weighed). Beat very well.
4 Do the same with the second egg, adding a second spoonful of flour. (The flour stops the mixture **curdling** when the eggs are added.)
5 Sieve the rest of the flour and gently **fold** into the mixture using a tablespoon.
6 Stir in any flavouring you have chosen, then place spoonfuls of the mixture into cake cases.
7 Wearing oven gloves, place the bun tin in the middle of the oven. Cook for 15–20 minutes. To test the cakes, lightly press a finger on top of cake. When cooked they should spring back.
8 Leave the cakes to cool, then decorate them.

To make glacé icing

Sieve the icing sugar into a medium-size bowl. Gradually add the water or juice until the icing is smooth but still fairly thick. Place a teaspoon of icing on each cake then create the face of your choice!

Some ideas for faces

Banana bars

Who said cakes weren't healthy? These tasty bars prove there is such a thing as a nutritious and delicious cake! They are not too high in fat or sugar and the bananas provide lots of energy and **nutrients**. Fruit and vegetables used to be used a lot in cake recipes, carrot cake being a popular example from New Zealand. Before starting to cook, ask an adult to help you.

Banana bars

Makes 8–12 bars

You will need:

Ingredients

- a little oil to grease tin
- 75 g soft margarine or butter
- 75 g soft brown sugar
- 2 eggs
- 225 g wholemeal, self-raising flour
- $\frac{1}{2}$ teaspoon cinnamon
- 2 large bananas
- 50 g walnuts

Equipment

- oblong (26 cm x 16 cm) or square (20 cm x 20 cm) cake tin
- brush for greasing
- scales
- large mixing bowl
- mixing spoon or electric mixer
- small bowl
- fork
- tablespoon
- sieve
- teaspoon
- plate
- chopping board
- small sharp knife
- oven gloves

What to do:

1 Set the oven to Gas Mark 5 or 190°C. Grease the cake tin using oil and a brush.

2 Place the margarine or butter and the sugar in a mixing bowl and beat together, using a mixing spoon or electric mixer until very light and fluffy.

3 Break one egg into a small bowl and beat with a fork. Add to the mixing bowl and beat the mixture with the spoon or mixer again.

4 Do the same with the second egg but this time add a tablespoon of the weighed flour at the same time. Beat the mixture again.

5 Sieve the flour and cinnamon onto the mixture. (The bran from the wholemeal flour will stay in the sieve, so just tip it into the mixture.) Using a tablespoon, gently **fold** the flour into the mixture until the flour cannot be seen.

6 Peel the bananas and place them on a plate, then mash them with a fork. They should be very soft and mushy.

7 Carefully stir the bananas into the cake mixture. Pour into a greased tin and smooth over the top.

8 Place the walnuts on a chopping board and chop them into small pieces using the sharp knife. (Take great care!) Sprinkle nuts all over the top of the cake mixture.

9 Wearing oven gloves, place the banana bars in the middle of the oven. Cook for 20–25 minutes or until the cake is well risen and springy when touched.

10 Allow the cake to cool for a few minutes before cutting into equal-sized bars.

Delicious cakes made from bananas!

Glossary

binding mixing ingredients together so that the dry ingredients are held by the wet ingredients

blast chilling getting foods cold very quickly

carbon dioxide a gas which is released from raising agents during the cooking of food products. As the gas is released it raises the food, leaving spaces in its place. This means foods, like cakes and muffins, have a light and open texture

confectioners shops selling sweets or sweet foods like cakes

creaming beating together fat and sugar to trap air bubbles

curdling what happens in cake-making if the eggs are added to the fat and sugar too quickly – it will look as if blobs of fat are floating around in it

dietary fibre material found in the cell walls of all plants including vegetables, pulses, fruits, cereals, nuts and seeds. Our bodies do not break down and digest dietary fibre but it makes our waste products soft so that they pass through our digestive system easily. Today dietary fibre is known as non-starch polysaccharide

folding mixing ingredients by gently turning one part over another

function the special purpose or job something has. Ingredients have a special purpose or job in food products

hygiene keeping free from germs and dirt

nutrients the chemical substances that make up food – they are protein, carbohydrate, fat, minerals and vitamins

nutritional value the type and quantity of nutrients in a food

raising agents substances that help food products rise when they are cooked. Raising agents are needed in cakes, muffins, bread and some biscuits and desserts

structure the framework of something. Without a proper structure food products could collapse. A cake made without any flour would be flat (and taste unpleasant!)

texture the way something feels; like ice feels cold, hard and smooth. We also feel the texture of food in our mouth. The texture of a biscuit may be crisp and crunchy but a cake's texture may feel soft and spongy

Further reading

Developing Skills in Home Economics. C. Connell, D. Nutter, P. Tickner, J. Ridgwell. Heinemann Educational Australia, 1991

Food Around the World. Jenny Ridgwell and Judy Ridgway. Oxford Universtiy Press, 1986

Home Economics in Action: *Food*. Judith Christian-Carter. Oxford University Press, 1986

Skills in Home Economics: *Food*. Jenny Ridgwell. Heinemann Educational, 1990

Index